Casey's

Dr. J. Helen Perkins
Photographs by Jamie Williams

Rigby
A Harcourt Achieve Imprint

www.Rigby.com
1-800-531-5015

This is Casey.
She loves her lamb.

This is Val.

She loves Casey's lamb.

Casey takes care
of her lamb.
Val helps Casey
take care of the lamb.

First Casey feeds
her lamb.
Val helps Casey feed
the lamb.

Next Casey walks
her lamb.
Val helps Casey walk
the lamb.

Then Casey washes
her lamb.
Val helps Casey wash
the lamb.

Casey and Val are wet!
It is fun
to wash Casey's lamb.

Casey and Val love the lamb.